CAN'T MAKE THIS SH*T UP

MARY LIZARRAGA & CHERYL CULVER

Contents

Introduction

Teaching. Molding the minds of future generations. Sounds inspiring. Sounds fulfilling. Then, the first bell rings. Before you can swallow your last first sip of coffee, your classroom is filled with thirty-eight, yes, I said thirty-eight young minds waiting for their learning to be inspired and fulfilled. No pressure, right?

Don't' get me wrong, teaching is exciting and rewarding. Seeing the face of your students when they succeed is a feeling that will never get old. But, teaching is also late-night grading, tons of emails, endless hours of professional developments (more affectionally known as P.D.) and marker stains on the new blazer you purchased for "Back to School" (which you have only owned for a week). Thank goodness for dry cleaning and Tide to Go sticks.

Before we get into the trenches about what teaching is really like, let's introduce ourselves and what led us to a career in education.

CHERYL

My story starts like so many others, I wanted summers off (just kidding). I really struggled with sticking to a major in college. To pay the bills I worked in schools in various capacities. The more time I spent in public education and the more heart-to-heart talks with my mom, I knew I wanted to carry on in her footsteps into the education field. Plus, like our mother always said, "It's job security, school districts are always in need of teachers". Where I've stood, this statement has been proven true year after year.

I was born and raised in Phoenix Arizona. I know, I know "At least it's a dry heat." Remind yourself of that while you stand outside during the afternoon for dismissal duty. Most of my primary and middle school education took place in inner city schools. I made the switch to a more affluent middle school my eighth-grade year. Let me tell you that was no easy transition. Uniformed white-collar shirts and navy-blue skirts were replaced with logo t-shirts and designer jeans. The footwear of choice: flip flops (with perfectly manicured toes). At 13 years old, I loved sweatpants and hated nail polish, so you can say, I stuck out like a clown at a funeral. Coming and going from one completely different neighborhood school to another brought light on experiences that I had never witnessed firsthand. Looking back, I can honestly say it helped me decide where I chose to be in my teaching career. I spent time working in various school districts with different demographics and always found my way back to my own neighborhood. This is where I would start my career as a Special Education Teacher. I've never once looked back. While I've encountered and overcome many personal and professional challenges since landing in this profession, I wouldn't trade those experiences for anything. Well, maybe for a winning lottery ticket!

This journey hasn't been rainbows and unicorns. In fact, most days are filled with rain clouds and gargoyles. Over the years I have seen the burn out that teachers feel after their first few years. I've also seen the resiliency in our veteran teachers that come back year after year with a smile on their face and a cup of heavily caffeinated coffee in their hand. It's been my goal to be part of the veterans who are IN IT TO WIN IT. I have thoroughly enjoyed all my years in education and look forward to many more. Hopefully, with better pay along the way. The students I've had the pleasure of teaching and the colleagues I've had the honor of working alongside has helped to shape me into the person I am today and strive for a better future for tomorrow. As a new mom, that mission has become even more vital. Now enough about me. Let's see what my sister has to say.

MARY

I, on the other hand, wanted summers off (not kidding). Let's just say teaching was not at the top of my list of career choices. I was supposed to be on stage, in the limelight, signing autographs. Growing up my interests and energy were towards the performing arts. I started dancing at 5 years old, and up until I turned 18, you'd find me front and center capturing the attention of any audience I could gather. Yes, I was the kid you'd find dancing in between tables at the local Piccadilly Cafeteria for my grandma and her senior citizen friend group. I took years of dance lessons, modeling, acting and performed at many events.

At 18, I became a mom. This is where my priorities took a shift. I soon realized that being on the Phoenix Suns dance team was not going to pay the bills. So, that audition was out! Is this when I decided to become a teacher you ask? Nope. In true fashion, I exhausted all other options throughout the years, such as theatre makeup artist, sign language interpreter, ballroom dance instructor, residential treatment counselor and pre-school teacher. It wasn't until I had "the talk" with my mom about what I wanted to do when I grew up, that I decided. The talks of becoming a teacher became more frequent. Teaching not only allowed for the flexibility I needed to raise a family, but it also provided me with the skills and structure I needed to raise a child.

Coincidentally, I also started my career in the school district I grew up in. The elementary that I was assigned to, was the same school I spent my kinder- 6th grades years. To my surprise, those who were once my teacher, were now my colleague. The hallway I used to walk as a student, was now the hallway I monitored as a teacher. My classroom, well it was the same one I spent time as a first grader in, and my neighbor, well that would be my sister's first-grade teacher! This alone, was an awesome way to begin my teaching career. Every year since then has only gotten better. Building continuous relationships and acquiring new ones has always been the best part of the job. The individuals I've had the pleasure *and* misery to learn from and work with have been a huge part of my journey and successes.

The path I've been on hasn't been easy, nor has it made me rich, but it's made me strong, so I wouldn't change it. As a teacher, I'm also a role model, so I'll continue to work, learn, struggle, fail, try-again and PREVAIL! My goal: pave a road for the future so that my daughters can feel courageous and will learn to grow, shine, and SUCCEED! I share this goal with my students so that they can feel the same.

Our reason for writing this book is to share with everyone what the classroom is like from our perspective. Beyond teaching. Teaching is more than colorful bulletin boards, hype pep rallies, and sweaty field days. Teaching requires a set of skills and mindset that will allow you to navigate through the individual needs of your students and the ridiculous encounters you'll experience with your colleagues. *Note to self: The goal is to de-escalate the situation (See Finish Line).* The stories that we share are only snap shots of what we have experienced as teachers, learned as educators, and felt as human beings.

As you will quickly notice, you will not be able to distinguish who is speaking in our chapters. This is done intentionally. Just so we're clear, we've both taught reading skills and can identify the various point of views. Our reasoning, though we've taught different grade levels, at different schools, under different leadership teams, AND with different coworkers, our experiences are essentially one in the same. We have been in this field for so long that we can tell what kind of day the other has had by the type of beverage we're holding (or the tone in our voice).

July-Warm-up

J uly marks the end of summer vacation and the start of a new school year. Positive energy fills the air and feelings of excitement race through me thinking about the new and familiar faces I am about to see. On the drive to school, my brain fills with fresh new ideas on how I am going to make this the best year ever. Then, I park my car and reality sets in quick. As I scan through our "Welcome Back" itinerary I immediately notice Wednesday, the half-day allotted (wedged in the middle of a pep rally and P.D.) for us to get our classrooms ready, set and organized for those thirty-eight students I will be greeting in five days' time. The rest of the scheduled activities are filled with ice breakers, team building, and, of course, MORE P.D. For you visual learners out there, I have provided a sample schedule below.

Monday-Meet and Greet	Tuesday-Data Day	Wednesday-Rally	Thursday-Principal Day	Friday-Back to School Walk
8:00-8:30 Meet and Greet	8:00-9:15 Reading Testing Data	8:00am-11:00 Back to School Rally	8:00-11:00 Principal Day	8:00-8:30 Breakfast and Check-in
8:30-11:15 Teacher Orientation (New and Returning)	9:15-10:45 Math Testing Data	11:00-12:00 Room Prep	11:00-12:00 Curriculum PD	8:30-10:00 Back to School Neighborhood Walk
11:15-12:00 TedTalk	10:45-12:00 Science Testing Data	12:00-12:45 Lunch	12:00-12:45 Lunch	10:00-11:00 School Training: Mitigation Plan
12:00-12:45 Lunch	12:00-12:45 Lunch	12:45-1:30 Room Prep	12:45-1:30 Curriculum PD Pt 2	11:00-12:00 Classroom Prep
12:45-1:30 TedTalk	12:45-1:30 Team Building Activity	1:30-2:00 Emergency Procedures PD	1:30-2:30 Lesson Planning	12:00-12:45 Lunch
1:30-3:00 Data Review	1:30-3:00 Team Planning	2:00-3:00 School Procedures P.D.	2:30-3:00 Room Prep	12:45-3:00 Team Planning and Grouping
3:00-3:30 Closing	3:00-3:30 Closing	3:00-3:30 Closing	3:00-3:30 Closing	3:00-3:30 Closing

Monday-The Meet and Greet

The first part of "Welcome back Week", is socializing in the cafeteria, because that's where we will be ALL week. The sounds of pleasantries and vacation stories being exchanged are muffled by the hyped-up songs being played over the intercom. There is no need for the "Electric Side" at 8:00am. However, credit is well deserved for the Culture and Climate Committee for their efforts in facilitating a warm and welcoming environment for our newbies that have no idea what is yet to come. Returning teachers are not fooled by this façade.

Picture your freshman orientation. We had our new incoming faces clutching their class schedules, picture I.D. hanging from their necks, and logo backpacks securely placed. Freshman were greeted by seniors who were handing out campus maps. Seniors didn't worry about their schedule until after syllabus week. Their school ID's were from sophomore year and in leu of a backpack they carried a pen and some scratch paper.

New Teacher Orientation is no different. Except, veteran teachers are not passing out campus maps. Instead, they're on one side of the cafeteria equipped with their worn messenger bags and thermal coffee cups. No I.D. On the other side of the café are the newbies equipped with their Starbucks cups and an organized teacher cart filled with a variety of flare pens wearing their lanyard around their neck. Little do they know this is the only week that will allow for their flexible morning routines. Coffee runs and organizational skills will soon cease to exist. But hey, they get credit for trying. Before there can be a flash mob dance scene, the principal gets on the mic to officially welcome us back and begin our meeting. And away we go!

Three hours later, after reading inspirational quotes, hearing personal stories of conquests, and watching a TedTalk video (the same one from last year), I am wondering how any of this applies to our teacher evaluations. Oh Crap, I'm already worried about student growth and the students haven't returned yet. Now I am even more anxious to get into my classroom, which won't be until Wednesday.

Returning from lunch, I took the opportunity to sneak into my classroom and avoid yet another inspirational video, after a while, they all sound the same. When I walked in, I groan at the sight that all my furniture has been moved to one side to accommodate for summer cleaning. I make a few mental notes of the classroom supplies that I need to ask the office staff for and sneak back into the cafeteria just in time for the ending credits. The art of perfect timing takes years of practice. Don't try this during year one of teaching.

The afternoon session was spent reviewing the same data that we were beaten with in May. As I look around the room the once happy and energetic faces of our newbies have been replaced with solemn looks of concern and buyers' remorse. Our veterans, on the other hand, have been saddled up since the beginning of June knowing what their new year would look like. After all, this isn't their first rodeo.

Our principal ends the day with commentary about how we are the right people for the job to meet the challenges ahead of us. I know it was meant to be inspiring and fulfilling but, considering he said the same thing last year to a different set of teachers, it falls flat.

Tuesday – Data Day

Charts, tables, and graphs OH MY! Data day. This is a time where teachers are inundated with numbers and percentages of academic growth made in EACH grade, level in EACH school, in the district. As the media tech prepares the big screen projector, our principal passes out hard copies of the 22 page (front to back) presentation. I look around the room and see the newbies armed with their flare pens, ready to take copious notes. To my left, I watch a veteran teacher fold the presentation in half and safely files it away in her messenger bag. At the podium, our principal delivers the somber "data" that our students are behind in Reading and Math. Like that was late breaking news. The sad realization is that our students are constantly falling behind due to various factors beyond the control of the classroom. We have always had struggles such as demographics, language barriers, and mental health. But this year brought on additional challenges such as a pandemic, school shutdowns, and teacher shortages. As a result, our students have fallen even further behind, and mental health needs have increased. Allow me to remind you that we have returned from a shutdown. During that time, teachers were expected to work miracles and most of the time, we did (two words: Distance Learning). We made Distance Learning as engaging and accessible as possible for all students. It was no easy task. We quickly became familiar with Zoom, Googleclassroom, Nearpod, Kahoot, and PearDeck. Not only did we learn these platforms, but we were tasked with teaching them to our students, online, over Zoom, with their cameras off. I prayed for the kindergarten teachers each day. Those prayers were shared with the middle school teachers who had Go Guardian alerts pinging at all hours of the night. That's the moment I deleted my school email app from my phone. A girl must get her sleep. We continued to sift through the piles of depressing data, and all I could think about was getting my bulletin boards ready. My theme this year will not be found on Pintrest. This is where my focus will lie until Wednesday morning.

Following our lunch break, one of the many specialists (I'm still not sure what their jobs are) had the bright idea to facilitate a team building activity. This year we played "Survivor", which was essentially the theme for teaching during a pandemic. We were given five challenges to complete across campus. Each challenge was meant to be completed as a team. My team lineup included three special education teachers, our school psychologist, and the speech Pathologist. Sounds like a winning combination, right? Wrong. You see, my teammates and I are trained to provide modifications and accommodations so that other individuals may succeed. We approached each challenge with the mindset of modifying and accommodating to fit our needs. Apparently, that wasn't the objective. When the rules of challenge #3 is to complete 5 push-ups (not 1), 20 jumping jacks (instead of 3) and a sprint around the track (we skipped this entirely), adaptive PE is not considered a winning strategy. In case you're wondering, we lost. The "Win" went to the special area teachers. This team consisted of PE, Art, Music, and Technology. They were 1 player short and still dominated. If you ask me, nobody stood a chance.

Next up, team planning. This is when we shake off our loss to the A-Team and gear up for our yearlong survivor challenges, Special Education. These challenges are for the highly qualified. Our obstacles include executing differentiated instruction across nine grade levels, hurdling through collaboration between all content area teachers, balancing behavioral support across campus, and refereeing mediations amongst parents and teachers. Our job description just switched to school gladiator. Game face on.

Wednesday-The Rally

L-E-T-S-G-O, Lets-Go, Lets-Go, L-E-T-S-G-O-, Lets-Go! (Back to my classroom because that's where my focus is.) As much as I want to be uplifting and enthusiastic just like the newbie next to me, I can't help but to prioritize setting up my classroom instead of dancing to "The Macarena". Some dances are meant to be forgotten. While settling into the bleachers, I scan the middle school auditorium and watch my fellow colleagues from our sister schools decked out in their school colors with pom poms, noise makers, and foam fingers as if we are at the Super Bowl. I quickly beeline to the complimentary breakfast table and before I can reach for the last sesame seed bagel, a coworker, plastered with face paint that reads Bulldogs, decides that this is the perfect opportunity to discuss the students on his class list that require related services. Being the professional that I am, I decide to continue our discussion while watching another face painted colleague take that last sesame seed bagel that was supposed to be mine. School hasn't even started, and I still can't eat. After finishing my conversation, I turn back around to the breakfast table only to see scraps and crumbs of left-over fruit, muffins, and bagels. Looks like I will be eating that granola bar (from the last day of summer school) I stuffed in my purse for situations like this.

I make my way back to the bleachers only to see my spot has shifted one up and two to the left. I was secretly trying to avoid sitting next to the math teacher. He's a nice guy and all, but math teachers are all about numbers with very little laughs. Not a good match for my personality. It's hard to get peppy sitting next to the guy who's worried about how they are going to teach linear equations this year. What are linear equations?

Our superintendent begins to strut towards the podium and silence the audience. As he, once again, says that the staff before him are among the best he has seen, mind you half of them are new hires, he proceeds to introduce this year's keynote speakers. Among them is a former student, a politician, and a fellow educator from out of state. All three shared personal stories of overcoming adversity while highlighting their triumphs along the way. Each story of success had several failures that were stepping-stones to obtaining their goals. Though I do question if the goal of the politician was to be arrested and forced to resign due to a sex scandal. But hey, what do I know about politics? I'm just a teacher.

After several rounds of applause and expressions of gratitude to our speakers, we are herded back to the bus to return to our schools. We have exactly two hours before our next P.D. During that time, we can work in our classrooms and eat lunch. Looks like I need to stock up on more granola bars.

By the time I was able to slap up two bulletin boards and scarf down a three-dollar vending machine meal, it was time to head back to the cafeteria to discuss school policies and emergency procedures. This piece is crucial. Our newbies need to know the importance of a school-wide evacuation. School-wide means EVERYONE. Not just the classrooms occupied by students. This includes the cafeteria staff, custodial workers, the nurse's station, and YES YOU, the teacher on her prep (you know who you are). Wednesday ends with us receiving our emergency folders equipped with evacuation maps and a flipchart with guidelines to follow in various emergencies. Knowing that these materials are not to leave campus, I am forced to return to my classroom and safely place them in their designated area. Entering my room, I am tempted to complete my bulletin boards and finish arranging my furniture. Where is the newbie next door you ask? Oh, I saw her hop in her car and toss her emergency folder in the backseat. It was urgent that she make it to her 4:00 o' clock yoga class. Odds are, she drops yoga by September.

Thursday-Principals Day

This is the day that our principal gets to present all day on topics such as duty and master schedules, the evaluation tool, committee assignments, mandatory reporting, and staff safety procedures. While each of these topics may seem mundane, I assure you they can make or break your school year. Let me explain. The duty and master schedules set the tone for the entire school year. If you teach middle school, you definitely don't want your prep first thing in the morning. Trust me when I say that a midday mental break is needed when you're dealing with hormonal teenagers. The before/after school duty station is as equally important. As a special education teacher, we are rarely given the choice of pleasantly greeting the students at the front gate. Where are we placed you ask? We're out in the middle of the field safely corralling students to their direct destination without any derailing. This duty cannot be assigned to just anyone. The person(s) responsible must be vigilant and fast moving. This duty requires spidey-like senses to be able to simultaneously prevent a fight, intercept trespassers and address the kindergarten student who fell in the mud. This confirms that I need to star in the next Marvel movie.

Before we can break for lunch, we must "volunteer" to be on a site committee. Choices include Assessment Committee, Safety Committee, PBIS, Culture and Climate Committee and PTA. Again, being a special education teacher, the choice is not ours. We are usually volun"told" to join PBIS. For those of you reading this that don't speak in acronyms, PBIS stands for Positive Behavior Intervention Supports. This is a fancy way of saying discipline and accountability. Due to our particular sets of skills, we are considered the experts in this department. Another confirmation that I be casted with my Marvel heroes. Since I have been told which committee I volunteered for, there is no need for me to linger with my colleagues and discuss the paly list for our next staff event with the Culture and Climate Committee. Looks like "The Macarena" and "Electric Slide" will live to see another school year.

Storytime "Birds of a Feather" Today I decided to treat myself and go off campus for lunch. Joining me is my "clique" (as my principal likes to refer to us as). I don't consider us "clicky". We are just a group of gals who get along, share some laughs, endure the hard times, and celebrate each other's milestones. Collectively I have known these ladies for forty plus years. What's referred to as a click, I label as a friendship. As we sit and chat about the year ahead, and years past, a group of newbies walk in, and I try not to make eye contact. The last thing that we want is for them to join our table in open discussion. As I look around the restaurant, I notice the lone empty table to fit their party lies directly next to us. Time to put the professional hat back on and be welcoming and inviting. Maybe I am not such a great fit for the Culture and Climate Committee after all. Of course, the one that is on the committee flags them down and asks them to sit. As the rest of us kick her under the table, the three newbies carry their trays over and seat themselves next to us. Our conversation quickly transformed from real talk and experiences to a cheerful questionnaire facilitated by the newbies. I can't tell you how many times I have been asked "So what does a Special Education Teacher do?" After I give her the rundown of my job description it's time to wrap up our table talk and head back for more serious discussions about state mandate reporting and staff safety procedures. A video on Blood Born Pathogens is exactly what I want to watch after eating a medium rare burger.

While the video plays on the projector, I find myself surveilling the room. As the newbies' eyes remained focused on the screen, my friend next to me is quietly creating a seating chart as I schedule out all of the first quarter's IEP meetings. It doesn't take a genius to know you must wear gloves when treating an open wound. Besides, don't we have school nurses for this reason? While we compare our quiz scores from the video, which I have aced ten years in a row, our principal sets up for his next presentation: State Mandate Reporting. This is no joke. Teachers must be aware and stay vigilant on the wellbeing of their students. Noticing the most subtle of changes can help save our students from the most serious of circumstances. All teachers take this seriously however veterans have a sixth sense in knowing when their student is in need. We are quick to question "Where did that scratch come from?" and "How did you get that bruise?". Building relationships with your students helps in ensuring they answer these questions honestly. When you don't know your students' names, they won't confide in you when they need it the most.

Friday-Back to School Walk

You might be asking yourself "What is a Back-to-School Walk?" The purpose is to connect with the school community and open lines of communication so that our students arrive on time and prepared for their new school year. The reality, the walk quickly escalates into a real-life jungle gym. We are dodging barking chihuahuas, avoiding stray cats, and maneuvering around countless ice cream trucks just to deliver a damn door hanger indicating when school starts. And to think, I could have been finished with my bulletin boards by now.

We quickly finish our route so we could be the first ones to the complimentary breakfast. We don't want to be left with cold eggs, bacon crumbs, and clumpy oatmeal. As we finish our food, we watch the newbies walk in with streaks of sweat, matted hair, and chipped pedicures. Apparently, they had the route with "Duke", "Hercules" and "Thor" the resident Pitbull's who protect their homes with great enthusiasm. I learned to avoid that route years ago. As we finish our breakfast, our principal announces that we will be starting our next school training: Mitigation Plan.

Mitigation Plans are new to all of us, regardless of your teaching experience. Remember, this is the year that we have returned from a national school wide shutdown amidst a global pandemic. Nothing is "normal". What do I mean by "normal" you ask? Well, normally we wouldn't need to worry about face masks, social distancing, and contact tracing. This year we needed to ensure that all students donned face coverings, followed the six-foot rule, and remained in their assigned seats. Yet again this is where my prayers go out to the kindergarten teachers. Can you imagine trying to manage all that with a room full of five-year-olds? No wonder we have a national teacher shortage. This sh** wasn't covered in "The First 100 days of School." During this training, we were provided with our supply of PPE (Personal Protected Equipment). The supplies included a box of facemasks, a box of gloves, face shields, hand sanitizer, cleaning spray, and district brand sanitizing wipes. All of which should last about a week. I can't tell you how often the students "misplace" their masks, how easily the gloves rip while trying to put them on, how frequently the students use hand sanitizer, and how gross their desks get after breakfast. Smart money is on me asking for more PPE before the end of the second week of school. Now that we are suited up for surgery, we can perform facelifts on our classrooms.

At last granted the gift of classroom time. I spent the time organizing student files, arranging desks, and finishing my bulletin boards. As is tradition, the need for reinforcements are called upon to carry out the near dead sewer roaches for proper burial. I guess this is a good time to break for lunch.

Lunch consisted of yet another peanut butter granola bar. Note to self: restock purse. My time was spent at the local dollar store purchasing last minute classroom supplies. One can NEVER have too many novelty pencils, neon sticky notes and multi-colored paperclips. Of course, the school supplies us with these items, however, their office supplies are best used towards the end of the school year. By then, I no longer care about being colorful, fun and festive. The novelty has worn off.

Before I get too excited thinking about the end of the school year, a colleague redirects my attention to team planning. All week, I have been able to zone in and out of presentations. This time, I'm the presenter. The reason for this initiative? As team lead, facilitating trainings is an expectation, one of the many expectations that are bestowed upon us. The time is spent reviewing and reinforcing district protocol when completing our extensive paperwork. Mind you, protocols change quarterly. We also establish our preliminary caseloads and schedule out tentative dates for reevaluations, annual IEP meetings and transfer meetings for those new students we are so eager to meet. I look over to our newest member (K-2

Resource Teacher) and it appears as though she will need to fit in an extra yoga class to deal with all the new information being thrown her way. Chances are I will be reviewing these protocols again before the end of the second week of school. Go Team!

As we close out the Friday before the first day of school, I am anxious to go to my next scheduled meeting: happy hour with my "clique" to debrief on this week's festivities and discuss any concerns for the upcoming school year. We're also placing bets on how long one of the newbies will last. My money is on her not returning from fall break. Miss Culture and Climate Committee is thinking she will stick around until December. Stay tuned to see which of us won the free coffee from Starbucks. I'm just getting warmed up.

August-Ready. Set. Go.

H ere we are in our second week of school. Let's recap on what happened last week shall we? First, and foremost, the emergencies stemmed from our kindergarten wing. These emergencies typically last for 2 weeks. Separation anxiety is real folks. Students being separated from their parents; parents being separated from their children and teachers being separated from their summer break. My job as a first responder is to relieve the tensions and deescalate emotions as quickly as possible. In one hand, I'm prepared with a detailed daily schedule to give to our parents so they may call us at the appropriate time to confirm that their child has eaten lunch and still has their hair intact. In my other hand, a box of tissues for the student who can't seem to catch his breath from the weeping and sobbing that he's experiencing from missing his mom. His mom hasn't left the room yet. As all this is happening, I felt the need to remind the kindergarten teacher that Labor Day is only 3 Mondays away.

One would expect that most of your attention would go towards the five-year old's who know nothing about school. Right? Wrong. We spend just as much time with our 8th graders, as we do our kinders, reviewing school norms and appropriate behaviors. Apparently, their brains are still frozen from the national shutdown which caused all students across America to catch amnesia. For the last year and ½, students fell into the habits of eating, sleeping, and completely ignoring anything academic. Those daily reminders of not eating, sleeping, or Face Timing during Zoom continue. These small examples are just a glimpse of what returning students are practicing now that we are back to in person learning. Man, I miss being able to turn off my mic and camera. In all fairness, teachers are not the same since Armageddon. As challenging as virtual learning was, nothing compares to the daily Survivor episode that is in person learning. Not only are we re-teaching school norms and academics, but we are also teaching our students to stay six feet apart, ensuring their masks cover their mouth and nose, and sanitizing every surface to Mr. Clean standards. Oh, and let's not forget contact tracing, maintaining google classroom for our quarantined students, and scheduling our formal observations. I'm ready to get kicked off this island.

Students are not the only ones struggling with the new norms. Amongst the staff it resembles the Hunger Games where we battle each other just to survive another day. First off, please do not write up students for not wearing their masks properly when you, yourself, have it hanging off your ear. Second, do not become frustrated that we are not quarantining the correct students when you are not following the seating charts that have been implemented. Lastly, do not complain about a student not tucking in their shirts when your daily uniform consists of flip flops and yoga pants. May the odds be ever in your favor enforcing rules that you do not follow.

Amidst the mitigation chaos, along comes benchmark testing. As previously mentioned, students have been out of a school building for more than a year. It's not rocket science to know that our students are not performing at grade level. It seems silly to put everyone through rigorous testing instead of focusing on the academic time that was lost and putting forth new energy towards the social/emotional needs of our students. While what I mention is common sense, the state requires the opposite. This just confirms the lack of knowledge and experience our officials have when making decisions about public education and a pandemic. In order to deal with these stressors, this month's professional development theme is "Self-Care". The foreshadowing of how this schoolyear will unfold is evident in our first PD. What is our objective? To create a self-care plan. Keep in mind, these plans are not the resources and care we need at school, but rather what we can do at home while we are lesson planning, grading, and responding to the emails we missed because we ran out of time during our contracted hours. Not sure what you're thinking, but I'm feeling better already, knowing that I can work another 3 hours from home utilizing these strategies.

Instead of listening to the feedback from our veteran teachers, which included ideas like designated prep time (not to be filled with meetings or subbing), sending out weekly schedule updates (as opposed to flooding my inbox every morning) and implementing a staff coffee/pastry bar (the stale chips and melted candy in the vending machine are not cutting it) we were told to craft our own at-home-plan and "pair share". This proved to be a challenge for some, especially my sister. It's a good thing we were paired together. Her self-care strategies are not-to-care. She'd rather pop a bottle while binging "Criminal Minds" on Netflix and save the teacher homework for a grade level PLC. Nothing screams RELEIF better than a drunk, sociopathic marathon. I have a feeling the crisis team would have been called and an immediate threat assessment might have been administered had she turned in her notes.

Storytime: "Careless". Following our P.D. on self-care I decided that I would put into practice some strategies. I wanted to give myself a spa day at home. I am talking a facial, pedicure, scented candles, and a glass or two of my favorite wine. Now because I am a dedicated teacher, I was also going to work on some lesson planning and schedule out any remaining IEP meetings that are due this month. Are you sensing an impending disaster? Your senses are keen. First, the face mask I used expired three months ago. This left me with a wet cement feel on my face that took 45 minutes to remove. I carry on retrieving my scented candles. I only have one left. I grabbed for it noticing that it's my favorite scent "Warm Vanilla Sugar" but couldn't find a lighter or matches anywhere. After an aggravating search in the house for an hour, I finally find one in my husband's junk drawer. ALL I really want at this point is to RELAX. Feeling triumphant I go to light my candle only to realize that the wick of the candle is gone! Trying not to feel defeated, I turn to gather all the proper tools to get my pedicure started. As I settled onto the couch to resume my "Criminal Minds" marathon, you guessed it, I knocked over my nail polish! The "Fire engine" shade of red I chose not only caused the living room to mirror a crime scene but was now the color of my face. After a forensic cleaning, I poured myself a pint of wine and hit play on Netflix. I'll try to relax next weekend. As for the lesson plans and IEP meetings? It'll have to wait until Monday.

As August comes to an end, I find myself both excited and dreading the remainder of the school year. I am dreading the number of referrals that will be written for improper mask use, the grades the students will receive come report card time, and the upset parents when students must be quarantined. On the flip side, I am excited to see my students again, work alongside my colleagues (out of a Zoom square) and have a sense of normalcy to my life. I must be prepared for what that "new" normal looks like in a pandemic. Ready. Set. Go!

September–September Sucks!

Please do not be alarmed by the title of this chapter. You must understand that September comes with turmoil. We have numerous excessive heat warnings, our days are doubled in hours, and there is only one school recess day at the beginning of the month. In essence, September sucks.

Let's talk about these excessive heat days. One requirement of a teacher is to be on duty. Picture this. Dismissal, the hottest part of the school day. You're outside surrounded by concrete and asphalt, engines roaring with sun rays beating on your head. One must not ignore the visible sweat stains peering through that neon-colored safety vest. This vest must be worn at all times. The reason, so that one may identify you as a staff member. The last time I forgot my vest, I was mistaken for "Stranger Danger" trying to snatch a student. Who knew I needed my vest in that moment for the principal to recognize me? I mean it's not like we didn't have my first observation for an hour that morning. My sole focus during dismissal is to try and avoid third degree burns while opening the car doors for our kindergartners and dodging the water bottle wars from our middle schoolers. The goal: to have the student population dismissed in T minus 15 minutes.

Storytime: "Hot Mess". The last thing that anybody wants to do is stand in the middle of the street in 110-degree weather. But here I am in full crossing guard uniform making sure our students and their families get home safely. In the thick of the stampede of pedestrians up walks a parent demanding an IEP meeting for their child tomorrow morning to clarify the progress notes that were sent home. If I am not mistaken, parent teacher conferences are scheduled for next week. Not sure what the rush is but we agree upon a scheduled time. After crossing that one student who is always last to leave campus, I make my way towards the front doors. I'm inches away from walking into air-conditioned bliss when a bus rounds the corner. Of course, bus number 55 has returned with all its passengers. I begrudgingly walk towards the bus as the driver opens its door and I ask, "What happened?". Turns out that was a loaded question. Apparently, our students forgot they were on a school bus and not at a grunge concert. Kids were yelling, standing on seats, and hanging various limbs out of the window. Scanning the crowd, I immediately identify some of our sparklers who are desperately trying to avoid eye contact. Still in uniform, I seat myself in the middle of those individuals and ask the driver to continue with the route. The atmosphere shifted from a jolly trolly to a cheerless carriage. After completing the last stop the bus driver thanked me and returned me to school. Arriving back to campus, I inwardly groan at the empty parking lot and dark front office. I resigned myself to the fact that I was wearing this uniform home and immediately got into my car. Cranking the AC while peeling off the sweat-soaked vest I try not to cry when I realized it was only Monday. Sigh.

We all know that summer days are long but when the observation cycles come around, they are that much longer. The first rounds of observations begin in September. Right after district benchmark testing and before the first set of parent teacher conferences. There is so much to prepare for, teachers begin their days earlier and end their days later. Observations are conducted on three separate days. Let me break this down for you:

Day 1: Pre-conference

During this time, we meet with our admin to discuss the lesson we are going to teach and review the data that supports the need for that lesson. We identify the standards being taught, justify the grouping of our students, and review the plan for reteaching should our students not grasp the concept the first time. Like that ever happens. The lesson I'm planning is one that I'm sure my principal has seen me teach before, several times. Not only have I worked under him for the past five years, but I've also delivered this same instruction anytime he's walked into my classroom. There shouldn't be any surprises here today. I arrive to his office with a copy of my lesson plan, student assessment data (to justify the need for the lesson), and the grouping for my kiddos. Having to explain that I intentionally placed my students into these subsets of groups based off their IEP goals seems silly considering my job title, but I'm rambling. This is the beginning act of the observation cycle. Get your popcorn and cotton candy ready for the main event.

Day 2: Observation

This is what you might call a dog a pony show. Our performance lasts for one whole hour. During this time, our pacing must be acrobat like precision. While normally, we might spend additional time reviewing previous concepts or practicing what we just learned, we are now juggling to fit in every element of the observation rubric, so we are not deducted points. What could go wrong? With everything mapped out so nicely, detours like a student refusing to participate and fire alarms blaring (the system was being tested) will only add to the Greatest Show on Earth.

As my students enter the room, I'm pleased to see that they have grasped our routine of retrieving their materials from their labeled folder (we have been practicing this for a month now) and immediately sitting at their assigned seat. For this lesson, we're reviewing identifying the main idea and supporting details of an informational text. After providing my direct instruction it's time for group work and student discourse. Each group was given a different passage (tailored to their reading level) and graphic organizers to map out their ideas. Like the proficient teacher that I am, I monitor their progress and participation. In doing so, I glance over, only to see one of my students sleeping while another was texting a classmate. With the magician skills I've acquired over the years, I managed to make the phone disappear before my principal could take notice. As for the sleeping student, the fire alarm took care of that! The show must go on.

Day 3: Post-conference

The post conference is designed to review with the Ringleader how the observation went. Suggestions are made on how to better engage my students (the one with his head down) and ignore the outside interruptions in order for my lesson to "flow" better (the fire alarm went off a total of four times). Suggestions are also provided on how to maximize the pacing. Apparently, I am expected to create additional minutes during the school day to set aside for remedial small groups. All in all, we set up another observation for the following week to ensure these changes were made. I would rather be the clown in the circus cleaning up after the elephants.

The feedback provided would be relevant had he remained seated for the entire lesson. Unfortunately, he missed the highlights of the program. Such as the fantastic small groupings I facilitated, the amazing dialogue initiated by my student who has struggled with sharing out loud, and the Kahoot exit ticket that I spent an hour (at home) creating. I guess I will have to extend my rehearsal for act two.

Our only school recess day was on September 6th, it's now the 27th. We have exactly 10 school days before fall break. These 10 days will include the requested encore to my observation and three days of parent/ teacher conferences. Say it with me… September Sucks!

October – HELLoween

A s the title states October is ALL tricks and NO treats. One would think that after having a week off, you come back refreshed right? Sadly, this is not the case. Whosever idea it was to start selling Halloween candy in the middle of September clearly should be slapped. Classrooms and hallways are littered with candy wrappers and the students start their sugar highs each morning that by the afternoon, they're mistaken for extras in "The Waking Dead." Not to mention, every social media platform consists of school pranks and challenges for our students to accomplish. For example, this month's challenge, Devious Licks. If you're wondering what a devious lick is, it's when a student accepts the challenge to steal something of school property. Big items such as soap dispensers, exit signs, and fire extinguishers are the most sought after. But would you believe that bathroom toilet paper also makes the list? After a pandemic, this really is devious. Teachers remained on high alert canvasing the classroom for missing staplers, tape dispensers and post-it-notes. Let's not leave out the occasional "scream" from a student in the hallway informing us of a flood in the restroom. This flood was "man-made" using paper towels that appear to be taken from the cafeteria.

Students committed these infractions with the aid of social media filters. Now I'm no detective, but the butterfly headbands and glitter backgrounds didn't bewilder me enough to call in the BAU (Behavioral Analysis Unit) to profile these individuals. I was able to identify exactly who the culprits were without any assistance. How? Well, I have a particular set of skills that I've acquired over the years. These skills allow me to predict exactly what's going to happen before it happens. So, when this happens, consider yourself caught!

Story time: "Caught Red Handed". I'm out in the hallway one morning making my way to another classroom, when I notice a group of three eighth grade boys leaving their class at the same time. I immediately was in pursuit. Now could it have been possible that their actions were innocent, and they just happened to be going in the same direction? Not a chance! After they rounded the corner to the bathroom, I lingered behind so I could listen for any signs of mischief. Trust me when I say it didn't take long. Twenty seconds later I heard the loud whispers of these boys coordinating something that clearly wasn't safe. After rounding the corner with my signature "What's going on here?" phrase, I spot the human pyramid of boy's inches from obtaining their exit sign trophy. Let me start by saying, they had it all wrong. With my experiences in cheerleading, the smallest person should be on top. So, why's "Jack" holding up "the Giant" in this tall tale? And if I remember correctly, tennis shoes, not Crocs, were the appropriate foot attire when attempting stunts such as these hooligans did. It was a matter of seconds before "Crocodile" Charlie slipped off Jose's shoulders and would face plant into Ricky. Can't they stick with the traditional game of "Capture the flag?" Attempting to hijack a school exit sign, one day of in school suspension. Performing an illegal cheer pyramid in the hallway, 3 days lunch detention. The look on their faces when they're explaining this nonsense to their parents, PRICELESS.

During the month of October not only are we gearing up to fight the candy wars that lie ahead, but we are also preparing for our first round of parent teacher conferences. At this time 1st quarter report card grades are due, IEP progress reports are updated, and fall sports are in full swing.

Parents are eager to talk with teachers about how their child's school-year has been going thus far. This is the opportunity for the teacher to communicate with families on how their student has participated in the classroom, performed on assignments and assessments, and allow families the opportunity to ask questions and provide insight on how WE can best support their child. This interaction is meant to be positive, productive, and solutions oriented. By taking this approach, trust between the teacher and families is built and will be maintained for years to come. However, we do have THOSE individuals who do not appreciate their role as a teacher and abuse their power instead of building strong relationships. Unfortunately, they would much rather go into full attack mode. Negativity takes full control of the conversation leading to unproductive encounters and more unresolved issues. Bridges are burned before they are built and yet they are asking "Why does the parent not support me?" I 'm no psychic, but I'm pretty sure that explaining to the parent that their child does absolutely nothing in class and is always causing disruptions was not the best sentence starter. In conclusion we do not want to end conferences with "The class was better when he was absent." (Shaking my head)

In all fairness, the pendulum swings both ways. I've had my fair share of parent no shows, have had to justify my teaching abilities, and have been insulted more times than I can count. As if it's my fault that their child has been absent and or tardy more than fifty percent of instructional days. It's no unsolved mystery as to why their child's academic performance is below grade level. One must be present to learn. A very simple concept that's too often overlooked. When parent denial kicks in, it just makes our job that much more challenging. Holding students accountable for their learning, behavior, and progress, is crucial. My teacher goal for my students is to promote self-sufficient practices, initiative, and ownership of their learning, their behaviors, and their choices. Without parental support and involvement in this area, it's a never-ending cycle of uphill battles.

I feel like this is a good opportunity to provide you with an update on our newbies. Let's just say we are currently in the process of looking for a new content teacher. To be fair, your first year of teaching should never have to include the words "pandemic" and "quarantine" but here we are. To be honest, I'm surprised she lasted as long as she did. Between mitigation plans, hybrid teaching, and implementing best practices, it's no wonder that teachers are leaving the classroom in search of a less stressful profession. Time to collect my Starbucks gift card!

The plus side to October is Fall Break! This is when I'm able to revert to sleeping in, watching the local news, and savoring that freshly brewed cup of coffee. Fall Break is my time of solitude. It's the time to travel, enjoy the weather and lounge around in a robe with a bucket full of buttery popcorn. The next thing I know, I blinked twice, and it's over. It's Monday morning and I've already had to cue 3 students about putting their costume back in their backpack. Halloween isn't for another 12 days. Let's take a moment to acknowledge that Halloween should be a day off when it falls during the school week or on a Sunday. It's nearly impossible to keep students engaged the night of or the morning after. One would think they would be sick of candy since it has been on the shelves since the beginning of September. No, they aren't. The day after Halloween turns into an extreme auction event with students bartering and exchanging their goods amongst themselves during class, recess, lunch, bathroom breaks, etc. It's only a matter of time before someone does not accept the Smarties they were given in exchange for a Snickers bar and all Helloween breaks loose. Thank goodness Thanksgiving break is only three weeks away.

November–Thankful for Vanilla Lattes

The month of November holds a special place for my sister and I. In addition to celebrating Thanksgiving, we also celebrate our birthdays. The whole month I am floating on cloud nine. Tis the season for layering. I break out with my leggings, tunic sweaters and knee-high boots to welcome the chilled air temperature that has begun. For my birthday, I am gifted (throughout the month) numerous gift cards to my favorite coffee place and the teachers' lounge is filled with baked goodies from those whose love for the Holiday season doesn't go unnoticed. The campus energy changes from frantic to fanciful as we all settle into the start of Winter.

The second quarter has begun. This is the time where we can teach, talk, and learn. There are no benchmark assessments getting in the way of student discourse. Teachers can facilitate literature circles without the stress of observation cycles. A Series of Unfortunate Events isn't just what we face on a daily, but it's the perfect text to hit all those reading strategies you've been reviewing for the past 4 months. During the weeks in November, I can't help but to reflect on what I am thankful for. Of course, the usual thanks go towards my most prized possessions, Mi familia. Without these individuals supporting me throughout life's journey, I don't feel that I would be the exemplary mom/wife/teacher that I am today. Yes, I described myself as exemplary, as this trait trickles into the classroom. Plus, it's my book, I'll use whatever adjectives I feel. Just like at home, in the classroom I am invested, committed and loyal to my students. I'm driven to provide the best instruction possible and have promised to give my all-in efforts of being an inspiration in my students lives. Sounds similar to what I strive for as a mother.

My students show their confidence in me every time they come forward with any problems they have, both in and out of the classroom. They're patient with me when I make mistakes and are the first ones to show support when other adults have me questioning myself and my abilities (You know who I'm talking about). Having strong, caring, trusting relationships with my kiddos fuels my fire for teaching. These same attributes also strengthen the connection that I have with my own family.

My thanks only get stronger when I think about the individuals that I share the front lines with. Without them, I probably wouldn't have lasted in this profession. Picture this scenario: I'm in the middle of a reading lesson when the phone rings, quite literally the call is coming from inside "the house". The office clerk is on the line informing me that one of my sparklers has hightailed it out of class and is roaming free. Did I mention admin is off campus? So, back-up is NOT coming from the top. The music teacher (who was on prep) offered to cover my class while I grab my next-door neighbor for this high-speed chase. Thankfully, she too was on prep. Walkie's in hand, we divide and conquer the campus. After numerous sweeps and exhausting patrols through the field and in the restrooms, behind the stage and in the library, we find him sitting at a random bench next to the sixth-grade building. Why the sudden stop? Well, he realized that his afternoon would involve an already scheduled annual IEP meeting with his mom. What did this mean for our roadrunner? This meant that he was to be isolated until mom arrived. Due to this stunt, mom will be arriving a lot sooner than scheduled. Once she's present, all new and relevant information will confirm that it's safe to say his least restrictive environment will still be restrictive. He'll also be suspended, effective immediately. Of all the consequences he faced, I'm sure the transport home was the most dreadful. After his departure, my colleague and I stop by the teacher's lounge for a much-needed break and a Pepsi. Looking at the clock, that break is going to last a mere five minutes. Without partners like these, surviving teaching wouldn't be possible.

Unless you haven't been paying attention, it's no secret that teaching is difficult. We all need that mental, emotional and, sometimes, physical support. These heroes brave the unknown all day, every day, and will never leave a teammate behind. They come prepared with caffeinated drinks, chocolate, and stress balls ready to provide whatever recon is needed. To my colleagues, I express my sincerest thanks and gratitude for having my back (during and after contract hours).

Storytime: "Forever Grateful". Amid teacher life, I also have a personal life that requires my attention. Sometimes, these two paths will cross and collide. That's exactly what happened to me. A few years ago, my assignment was the K-5 Emotional Disability (ED) classroom. During this same year, I was faced with responsibilities of being a care giver. I volunteered for both roles without hesitation. However, I never quite prepared myself for the tsunami of emotional and physical strain that I was about to endure. My days consisted of students hitting, screaming, crying, and cussing me out because they did not have the skill set to self-regulate and maintain their own personal feelings. My nights were filled with bedside manner practices, hygiene support, and pretty much zero sleep. Those who were aware made every attempt to comfort, feed, and distract me so that I can make it through the day, knowing what I was up against at night. I remember one specific morning, dragging myself to the classroom, I turned the corner of the hallway to see my friend with her arms out asking, "How's Nana?" My reaction: I buried my head in her chest so that I could cry it out. Knowing what my immediate needs were at the time, she held me tighter and cried with me. No words needed, just a hug. This one small genuine gesture will forever reside with me. Having a support system at work during those trying times got me through the months ahead so that I could mourn the loss that was inevitable and continue to persevere in the classroom as an educator.

On the lighter side of things, I'm also thankful for the partners in crime that have shared the laughs, shenanigans, and speeding tickets we've come across (to be fair the light was yellow).

In short. Thanks, a LATTE!

December–Hello Holidays

Ahh December. The time of year where we can start counting down the days until a two-week vacation. Before we can prepare for our break, we must shift our gears towards winter benchmark assessments. It's the end of the second quarter, which means it's time to analyze the amount of growth our students have made since August. Of course, they're all going to be on grade level and will have shown mastery in every concept. I mean, why wouldn't they? It's not like we haven't had any interruptions to instruction such as quarantines and shutdowns, right? Obviously, we ALL know the answer to that question. When I received the anticlimactic benchmark results, it felt disheartening. The academic growth I anticipated my students to make was lower than expected. I know that it's not my instruction to blame nor is it my students' lack of effort. The factors involved were out of anyone's control. Homelessness, hunger, illnesses, and poverty are to name a few. We, as educators, are constantly engaging in an uphill battle. There are many obstacles thrown our way that it becomes more difficult to navigate through the curriculum pacing guide effectively. I'm outnumbered when going up against such enemies. Put it this way, I 'm about to change my last name to Custer.

Whether we hit those benchmarks or not, celebrating student successes happen on a daily. I mustn't forget the growth my students have made both socially and emotionally. As tough as it's been for me, I know that it hasn't been a walk in the park for them. Much like adults who worry about their responsibilities, I've had students in that same mind frame. Fifth graders responsible for cooking, cleaning, and raising their siblings so that parents can work those extra hours during the night shift. Eighth graders who've had to catch the city bus by 5:00am and third graders whose only source of food is what's provided by the school. My celebrations go out to these kiddos. Not because they've scored "proficient" in math reasoning, but because they show up to my class, every day, with a smile on their face ready to learn something from me. Little do they know I'm learning from them. I think to myself, if they're able to push through and overcome these obstacles, well then, I can overcome my own. Their strength and resilience inspire me to continue to be the best version of myself and not give up on anything.

This month my focus is not on assessment scores or progress monitoring goals. Instead, I concentrate on ensuring that I am fully immersed in all the holiday activities. I volunteer to judge the door decorating contests, wrap Secret Santa gifts, and don my ugliest Christmas sweater (the one that lights up). My favorite part is the potluck. This ain't just any potluck folks. Teachers are serious about their holiday dishes. The competition for the best cookies, cakes, and pies mirrors an episode of "Extreme Cupcake Wars". I never knew there were so many variations of a fruit cake before. Yet, there doesn't seem to be one that I like. The recipes displayed in the lounge are treated like a lesson plan for an observation cycle. The preparation is intense as there is no room for modifications. I, on the other hand, can provide numerous suggestions on how to improve the fruit cake. (As I discreetly wrap it into a napkin and toss is at my earliest convenience).

Storytime: **"Party at the Principals". Being invited to the principal's house is like finding the golden ticket in a candy bar. My first thoughts, are of course, I wonder what her house looks like? Her home must be cleaner than mine. I bet she has an interior designer! I hope I don't break anything. Preparing for the party, as if I was going to the Grammy's, I'm stressing about my outfit.**

I obviously cannot show up in my daily attire. This is my time to shine and look the complete opposite as I did last Wednesday. What's the secret to this Cinderella transformation? Heels of course because this is something that I NEVER wear to work. Coordinating with my clique, we decided to stagger our arrival times. I was about to make my grand entrance when I remembered I forgot the White Elephant gift! Shifting gears, I made a mad dash to the nearest CVS. Did I mention it was a week before Christmas? The store was severely picked over. I had to quickly get creative. I grabbed the last gift bag (one of the handles was broken), some tissue paper (mustard yellow will have to do), and the last Christmas themed popcorn tin available (yes, the can was dented). I threw the items into the gift bag and promptly made my way back to the party. I was forty-five minutes late by this point. While entering my principal's home, I walked into a spirited game of Pictionary. The infamous special area teachers were up against our kindergarten teachers. This particular round the P.E. teacher was drawing, however, his illustration resembled drawings from a football playbook. I can't help but to linger and see who can guess what it is that he's drawing. After several attempts from his teammates, the timer goes off giving the kindergarten team a chance to steal. After a quick huddle, they shout out in unison "Old McDonald!" The special area teachers groan and hesitantly admit defeat. As the night progressed, I become increasingly aware of how much I hate heels. By this time, my feet were sweaty, ankles swollen, and my pinky toes were begging for some relief. I make my way back into the living room (without tripping this time) and begin to visit with the school psychologist. Just as I convinced her to stay a while longer, I spotted the mud stains in the white carpet. Oh No. Who's responsible for this? I've got to warn them. My eyes are focused on scanning everyone's shoes as they walk by me. After 20 minutes of staring at the ground analyzing the

cleanliness of each shoe that walked past me, it dawns on me, I haven't checked my own shoes! Earlier that evening, while outside, my heels sunk into the mud. In a flash I recall the countless times I grabbed onto a colleague's arm to lift me out of the sink hole I was creating. I needed to make a quick exit. I devised a tale of needing to get up early for a very important appointment (on a Sunday morning) I bid farewell to those in my eyesight. Ensuring I was not spotted as the culprit of the stains, I stashed my shoes in my purse before leaving. I just hope I get invited to next year's party

The last week before break our conversations consisted of last-minute holiday planning and reminiscing about our holiday party. Apparently, my dented popcorn tin was not the worst gift. That honor goes to whoever wrapped a single packet of hot chocolate for me to open. Word of advice, splurge for the brand with marshmallows next time. In other news, no one has confessed to the mud stains. I really hope they get to the bottom of that mystery soon. The remaining hours before Christmas break feels like walking "The Green Mile". I pray that we can get to our dismissal bell without incident. After a few minor hiccups (a fire drill, food fight, and lost backpack) the clock strikes 12:00pm (yes it was a half day) and we are free. I dash to my car and zip out of the parking lot faster than you can say "Figgy Pudding". Hello holidays!!

January–Back in Action

I'm not exactly sure when it happened, but winter break is officially over. I'm sitting in my classroom still trying to recover from New Year's when the bell rings. This is the universal signal to the start of every school day. Oh, how I wish the intercom system were still broken. Students are still in vacation mode with their hoodies wrapped around their heads wearing questionable foot attire. (For the record, slides are never allowed) As for me, I stand before them pushing the dress code limit myself wearing an oversized sweater trying to hide the yoga pants that will be frowned upon if I cross my principal. Messing with a zipper or buttons of any kind was not an option today. It's a quarter to 9:00am and I'm already late in starting today's reading lesson. This works out well considering my students are just as late getting to class. There is an unspoken agreement today to ignore our tardiness. I throw my coffee in the microwave and finally start the day. When is our next break?

January is a strange time in schools. The school year is technically halfway over but there is still so much to accomplish. The second round of parent teacher conferences are just around the corner and trainings for state assessments have begun. Every year it's the same thing. Do not give students answers to the test, keep the environment secure and ensure that all students have the proper accommodations available to them. This can all be communicated in an e-mail as opposed to a 2.5-hour training, but I digress. I head over to the media center, computer in hand, and begin to diligently take detailed notes as my principal reads aloud EVERY slide. My note taking skills have quickly diminished. One window of my computer is opened to the training module (on mute) while I finish writing an IEP for tomorrow's meeting. I have it timed perfectly to click back when I need to advance to the next slide. I have the answers written down for our quiz from six years ago. This is multitasking at its finest.

We've been back in session for three weeks now and instead of addressing academic standards, I'm addressing ridiculous behaviors. Why must students wait until they return to school to pierce themselves? Why can't they have the "I'm better than Lebron fight" on their own basketball court? And who said that flying your drone in Algebra was a good idea? You may think I'm exaggerating but these are all real questions I've had to ask myself. These are the days that my sanity is pushed to the limits. To be clear, I'm not the only one a heartbeat away from a mental breakdown most days. It's a shared phenomenon around the campus. For example, my next-door neighbor's stories would shake you to your core. Move over Stephen King, Pennywise is no match for middle school angst. One day during her math lesson, a student decided it was a good time to have a snack. He proceeds to take out leftovers from breakfast, it's the middle of the afternoon at this point. As he unwraps his breakfast pizza, the classroom begins to resemble a Shark Week feeding frenzy. All attention turns to him as he starts to share his backpack buffet. As it tends to happen, the food runs out, the tensions run high, and a water bottle fight ensues. Where's my neighbor during all this? Well, Newbie Nancy is dutiful standing in the front of the room sticking to her pacing guide and meeting the lesson's objectives. I would say she was the ONLY one participating in this lesson, however, strait "A" Adam was on point and correctly answering questions in all this madness. I am almost certain this gave Newbie Nancy a false sense of accomplishment.

On the flip side two doors down to the left, Veteran Vincent is having a different kind of day. On our lunch break, he broke down his entire morning and by the end I needed a nap and a drink. As he was introducing his new unit about Colonial America, one student shouted out that "if Donald Trump were president during that time, they would have had electricity and no issues with witches". I'll wait while you roll your eyes. As Vincent tries to refocus the lesson topic, shouts of "you're stupid" erupted and two boys started posturing up ready to fight. What did Veteran Vincent do? He didn't have to do much. A mere glance and two steps forward signaled both students to sit down and stop with the nonsense. He continued to eloquently explain that was not how electricity was invented and witches were in fact NOT real. He calmly reminded the class of our school wide expectations and simply said to the two rivals "we'll continue this lesson during recess." Veteran Vincent may seem detached, but that's the furthest from the truth. The truth is, Vincent has been at this for 27 years now and has mastered the art of classroom management and community. While it may give the illusion of detachment and lack of emotion, nothing could be further from the truth. Veteran Vincent may not wear his heart and feelings on his sleeve, the community he builds inside his classroom reflects just how much he cares about the safety and well-being of his students. Not all heroes wear capes.

Storytime: "Road to Suspension" It was a relatively slow day in the neighborhood. Time was flying by and before I knew it, lunch time had arrived. As I retrieved my hot meal from the microwave preparing to eat, my phone rings. Just as I'm about to answer, my principal walks through my classroom door with several middle school students in tow. I immediately put my food to the side surrendering the idea of a hot lunch or having a lunch at all. I answer the phone and the secretary, immediately begins to fill in the blanks. Apparently one of our seventh graders channeled her inner mafia side and began an organized crime syndicate. With my principal, 3 students (who I dismissed fifteen minutes ago) were the hired help. As soon as they sat down, they began to sing like canaries. Turns out, they were each paid one hundred dollars in exchange for ensuring protection.

As I am listening to this plot unfold there are so many unanswered questions brewing in my head:

Question #1) Why does a seventh grader feel the need for protection? Come to find out, social media played a huge factor in this organized crime attempt. These ladies were apparently promised to the same boy without their knowledge of each other. In the attempt to proclaim her frog prince, Vengeful Vicky decided to call out Wicked Wendy and created a meme with her school picture and posted it in a group chat. These days, those are fighting words. The entire 7th grade class had viewed and commented on this meme in under 15 minutes. This meant war for Wicked Wendy!

Question #2) Where is the Frog Prince in all this criminal activity. Isn't he the one who is concealing both of their identities? What are the ghosting signs in middle school? Would it be appropriate to introduce the book "He's just not that into you?" This seems like a lot of trouble to go through when they won't even sit together at lunch.

Question #3) Where in the world did she get three hundred dollars? Most middle schoolers spend their birthday money on new shoes, phone accessories, clothes, and gaming gear. But not Vengeful Vicky. She is advanced. While average teenagers swindle their money away on material items, Vengeful Vicky was planning for her future success in 7th grade. Her level of criminal thinking mirrored that of The Godfather. Maybe one day she will make me an offer that I can't refuse.

As January comes to an end, I note how many weeks we have until spring break and begin crossing them off the calendar. Reminding me of a pandemic, this month has been the COVID Express. We've had to quarantine at least one class in every grade level and have been short staffed every day due to teacher illness or burn out. The challenge ahead is ensuring that our students are prepared for state assessments to the best of our ability despite the pandemic. It's the reality that we've been living in. We're back in action! February should be interesting.

February—For the Love of Teaching

After reading the chapters thus far, you've probably been asking "Why did I get into teaching to begin with?" Well, I'll give you my top five reasons:

1) *Wanting to make a difference*

As cliché as this may sound, it's true. I became a teacher in the neighborhood I grew up in because I wanted to give back to my community and represent. I was able to create a bond with my students because I knew where they were coming from, literally. I wanted to show my kiddos, that no matter what their circumstances, they could grow up and be as successful as they wanted to be. I want my students to have the mentality that just because they don't live in a fancy house or have limitless finances, their chances of success are still great. Challenging my patience and commitment, students have questioned if I'd come back. My answer to them is "I'm here now, aren't I?" I accept that challenge every day. I come to work with a smile on my face and forgiveness in my heart for yesterday's antics. I'll continue to give my all… because they're worth it.

2) *Job Security*

Teaching is job security. As my sister says, "We make other professions possible." Without teachers there wouldn't be doctors to treat us, lawyers to represent us, and first responders when we need them the most. These are just a few examples of the careers that, we as teachers, encourage our students to strive for. The list is endless. Ever notice that musicians, movie stars, and athletes will most often mention that one individual who inspired them? Well, that's me. I'm that teacher, coach, and mentor. I'll never take the spotlight or credit for their success, nor will I ask for a parade and awards. I will, however, be their biggest cheerleader and supporter. So long as teaching remains a profession, all other professions will continue to exist. No better job security than that.

3) *School Calendar*

Yes, the school calendar is a legit reason I became a teacher. Who wouldn't want the occasional school recess day or two weeks for winter break? This is especially true after I became a parent. I wanted to be home with my kids when they were and enjoy the flexibility of participating in school events. While I don't agree with the "it must be nice to have summers off" nonsense, the breaks we do have are a bonus. I mean, what other profession allots these?! All I'm saying, is that if you wanted a reason to become a teacher, the school calendar fits in the "pro" column.

4) *Variety in a Day*

I honestly couldn't imagine myself sitting in a cubicle doing the same thing day in and day out. No shade to those professions but it's not for me. While I've given you examples of class drones, fights, and pop-up piercing parlors, there is so much more to imagine. Celebrity status is my favorite. This is when random students come up to me, hand me a sticker and tell me that I'm their favorite teacher. Most of these kids have never been on my class roster, but the feeling is amazing! Kids are also brutally honest and there is no way to predict what they'll say next. You're either in for a sweet compliment or some constructive criticism. The unknown is what makes it fun.

5) *Intangible Rewards*

The last reason on my list are the intangible rewards. These rewards you can't reach out and touch. It's NOT about the Benjamins when it comes to teaching. The rewards are the smiles I get from my students when they master a concept or the joy in their voice when they've been accepted into the vocational school they've dreamt of. I especially love when a returning student stops by to see me, say hi and explain all the great things they're achieving. These tight bonds keep me going back year after year. In my opinion, no other profession is as emotionally rewarding as this one.

Storytime: "Beyond Teaching" The love I have goes beyond the classroom. It was the beginning of my third year of teaching. Our school counselor had sent out a school wide email asking for any donations possible to help a former student in need. The former elementary student was now a high school student and needed baby items. She was about to be a new mommy. A sophomore in high school and instead of focusing on the latest fashion trend for herself, her responsibilities were now to dress, diaper and feed the baby she was about to give birth to. I was not familiar with this specific student since she was already in middle school when I began teaching at the elementary school she had attended. I approached the school counselor asking for more details of the former student and what exactly it was that she needed. The counselor informed me of the situation, and it turned out, this child needed everything that came along with having a child (with zero family support). I immediately poured my heart out into helping this girl. As a teen mom myself, most everything about her story I was familiar with, however, I had family support, so feeling "alone" was not something I could relate to. She was alone and I wanted her to know that somebody cared. That semester, the exchange and delivery of baby items that I donated were handled through our school counselor. I never met this girl, but I cared for her as if she were one of my students. I showered her with diapers, onesies, bottles, and gift cards that semester. By the end of November, the need for a crib at my house was over so I donated that too. With never meeting this girl, my hopes were that I was helping her meet her needs. Once we returned from winter break, I learned that she had moved to live with an aunt of hers. This gave me comfort in knowing she was no longer alone, and I could stop rummaging through my daughter's things to donate. Fast forward three years. At the same elementary school, I check my mailbox in the teacher's workroom to find an envelope addressed to me. In it, a thank you card with a picture of a beautiful little girl who looks about three years old. She's sitting on the lap of a young lady who appears to be her mom. On the back of the picture, it read: "Thank you so much for everything. We will never forget you." The picture was signed with both her and her daughter's name. My heart sank while my eyes welt up. I could finally put a face and name to the girl, and her baby, who I had thought about for so long. This is why I teach.

You see, teaching goes beyond the confines of the classroom. Those four walls may be where the relationships and bonds begin, but it extends so far out that students you never taught will feel the impact. Between the school calendar and wanting to make a difference, I can honestly say that everything I do is for the love of teaching.

March-Spring Fever

The first two weeks of March is non-stop action. There is so much to get done in a short amount of time due to Spring Break. We are in the throes of training for state assessments and preparing for our final round of parent teacher conferences. The weather outside is warming up and so are student behaviors. We are barely two days in and here I am already sitting through another training on testing responsibilities and compliance protocols. Let me clarify. State assessments happen once a year at the same time. I have been teaching for seventeen years. I'll let you do the math on how many times I've administered this test. If you guessed seventeen, kiss your brain! The protocols haven't changed, but the name…they still haven't gotten that one right. For those of you who remember the Iowa Test, this is what I am referencing. Protocols are still the same since 86', I just can't remember if we're calling it the Stanford 9 or not? Chances are that by the time you are reading this, the name will have changed…again.

You know how I mentioned that student behaviors were warming up? Here's an example. It's recess for our third and fourth graders. It's a beautiful partly cloudy day with a light breeze in the air. A nice break from the previous day's high of 90 degrees. One would assume that it would be a relaxing and enjoyable time for monitoring recess duty. No, of course not. One of my fourth graders decided to go WWE on some girls by placing them in a choke hold and slamming them to the ground. I mean he was running around picking girls at random and repeating this for the entire length of recess (15 minutes). Since it wasn't my scheduled duty, I was unaware of the havoc that was occurring on the field. Instead, I was informed the following day because NO adult saw this. It's perplexing to me. Due to COVID mitigations our grade levels are separated at recess. Meaning when one grade level is using the playground and basketball court, the other has full reign of the athletic field. When you're assigned a zone, please, tell me how this happens?! It's an elementary school field, not the NFL. Unlike the NFL, we don't have the staffing to support the number of students running around campus. We would love to have more adults available during lunch and recess. More adults on the field would mean more supervision, which means, less opportunities for wrestling matches. Where I've taught, the typical teacher/student ratio is 1:36. Multiply these two grade levels by eight classrooms. The total, 288 students. Who's watching all these kids during recess you ask? Their teacher(s) of course, however, they too consider themselves at recess. With a playground ratio of 8:288, you're already out numbered, now is not the time to congregate and discuss each other's Amazon wish lists. These last three days before spring break are going to feel like an eternity.

We made it!! Yes, that sentence deserves two exclamation points. Nine glorious days of peace, serenity, and no schedules to abide by. Unlike a lot of my colleges who are blessed to experience the extravagant spring break vacations that one dreams about such as Hawaii, Jamaica, Europe, and Asia, I prefer the spontaneous trips to Target, unlimited access to Netflix, and food on demand with Postmates. And if I were to get a wild hair, I might even log onto AirBnB to check their weekend rates. I'll hold off on committing to anything, I mean I don't want Ashley (the Target cashier) to think that I have abandoned her. It's not like I can't afford these lavish vacations or that I don't deserve them. I choose to spend my time at home unpacking my kitchen from when we moved (5 years ago), getting caught up on laundry (because it never ends), and organizing my closet (my sister loves when this happens). Plus, I am a family of four. We have a hard enough time deciding what to eat for dinner. By the time we settled on a destination, vacation would be over. Instead, I choose to spend my abundant teacher's salary promoting our local economy. You're welcome!

Returning from spring break, I feel just as exhausted as my neighbor does who returned home from Germany last night on the Red Eye. I spent two hours meal prepping. While others are sharing pictures and trinkets from faraway lands (I saw it all on Facebook), I'm unpacking my Dollar Spot purchases for my reading centers. Maybe I do need to rethink my idea of how I vacation after all.

To top it off, March is where we see the most referrals for special education evaluations. Why you ask? Well, they want to ensure they make that sixty-day deadline. I guess these individuals think that we can also walk on water to be able to test upwards of thirty students before the last day of school.

March madness for teachers has nothing to do with filling out a bracket of college basketball teams. Instead, it's a list of students who, various individuals, have requested for a special education evaluation. Some people think an IEP is the solution for everything. Three letters apparently can solve any problem short of world hunger and cancer. When a student is misbehaving? Give them an IEP. When a student is failing their classes? Give them an IEP. When a student is chronically late to school? Give them an IEP. I don't even think Oprah would hand out that many IEP's and that woman gave away cars!! It seems by this point of the school year; common sense stops existing and easy, simple fixes are expected. I get that we are all tired, but we can never stop being teachers. If students are struggling, we are their first line of defense. I can't tell you how many students have been referred for an evaluation where ZERO interventions were documented or tried. Let me make this clear, putting a label on a child for an IEP is not something that should be taken lightly. It is, in most cases, a commitment and need that spans the child's entire school career. An IEP is not a reason for a kiddo's challenges but rather a detailed resource on how to help that kiddo succeed. Just because a kid continues to chew gum, hasn't memorized multiplication facts, or is chronically late for class does not mean they automatically get an IEP.

Storytime: "Free Consultation" Waldo is a kiddo who fits the general education teacher's description of a student who supposedly needs special education. Waldo's a sixth-grade boy whose interests include playing Pokémon and collecting Hot Wheels. Like most middle school boys, Waldo is often grumpy in the morning, but his mood picks up after breakfast. He's at school on time every day and is a responsible and loving older brother to his two younger siblings. Waldo is very tech savvy and is always willing to help others (adults and students) with their IT needs. It's no surprise that being hounded about having his shirt tucked in at 8:30 in the morning starts his day off wrong. I'm not saying don't hold him accountable but maybe start with a "Good Morning, how are you today?". Waldo really is a pleasant kid to get to know. I keep all of this in mind when his teacher approaches me every day about his need for an IEP. My responses to her when she is delivering her reasons sound much like this: Teacher: He continues to chew gum in class. Me: What are the consequences for the other students who do the same? My understanding is that lunch detention and a phone call home are the school wide policies for this behavior. Inner voice: *I'm sure he isn't the only kid to constantly chew gum*. Teacher: He refuses to tuck his shirt in. Me: What happens with the other kiddos that need constant reminders? Have we talked to anyone about getting him longer shirts that can be tucked in? Inner voice: * The girls are the worst who intentionally wear short shirts*. Teacher: He continues to tap his pencil. Me: Is he the only one that does that? Have you tried replacing his pencil with a small fidget? Inner voice: * I can point out six different students who do the same thing all day long*. Not to take away

49

from his behavior needs but an IEP is not going to cut it. If this was the criteria for a child needing an IEP, 90% of all middle schoolers would have one. Not to sound like a broken record but it really comes down to relationships. If an outsider looking in can't determine who's the student or the teacher based on behaviors, then there's a problem.

With the abundance of state testing trainings and evaluation referrals, no amount of four-leaf clovers will change my luck around. By the end of it all Spring Fever has SPRUNG!

April – Testing in Full Bloom

N ow that I am settled into my work week routine, it's go time for state testing. Per our trainings, I am diligently removing anchor charts from my walls, arranging my desks into straight rows, and taking inventory of my pencil and scratch paper supplies. I proactively printed out the district provided trouble shooting guide for the inevitable technology glitches that are going to occur. This tends to happen when most of the student body are logging into the same testing app all at once. Our poor IT guys really get a workout this time of year. Teachers and students enter a robotic stage for two straight weeks. Students go through the motions of turning on their computers and entering the necessary credentials to access their assessments. Teachers are on auto pilot and read the same testing direction scripts every day. Hands down this is the most tedious and boring time of the school year.

We've been testing for approximately 2 weeks now. You're probably wondering why testing takes as long as it does, well, let me explain. State testing consists of 6 sections responsible for assessing all students enrolled in school. This includes both public and charter schools. Students are tested in Reading, Written Expression, Mathematics and Science. Depending on the student, one section can last all day. Why all day? Well, technology glitches for one. Students are constantly kicked off the testing website causing them to log back in numerous times. Screens become frozen, which means students must again, log back into the website. The most aggravating technology glitch, computers die! This means we're on a scavenger hunt to find the correct charger for that later modeled

Chromebook (which doesn't seem to exist). Another reason for an all-day test marathon, the frequent bathroom breaks. Nothing screams avoidance louder than a middle schooler whose name is written on the sign-out sheet 12 times. We've only been testing for 30 minutes.

This is a good time to remind you that I'm a special education teacher, so testing for me and my students in my classroom looks a whole lot different. My students require individualized accommodations in their testing environments. What does this look like? It's small group testing with frequent breaks allowing for extended testing time. This means we'll be testing ALL day because my students cash in on their extended breaks. Students are also allowed the use of headphones so that the test directions may be read to them. Sounds like a simple enough accommodation, but it's not. You see, not only are we experiencing the technology struggles as described in the previous paragraph, but we're also trying to decipher which (district provided) headphones will not sound like Darth Vader. What I have mentioned so far only has to do with state testing. I have yet to describe AZELLA.

The AZELLA assessment measures the language proficiency of students identified as potential English learners as determined by the Home Language Survey. The test consists of four sections: reading, speaking, listening, and writing. AZELLA takes just as long as our state assessments to complete. Accommodations are essentially the same and protocols mirror our other tests. The main difference is the speaking portion. As the title suggests, students are expected to verbally respond to prompts. This obviously cannot be done in a group of any size. Instead, students must complete this portion 1:1 with the testing proctor. Students enter a secluded area with the proctor and use a telephone to answer their questions. The average time for a student to complete this portion is twenty minutes. Doesn't seem like a long time, right? Break out your calculators. With an average time of twenty minutes and needing to test 210 (K-8) students what is the total time needed to complete this section? I'll give you some extra think time before we continue. Final answer is 4,200 minutes. Feel free to convert this number to hours on your own time. Simply put, special education teachers are not exaggerating when we say that we spend a whole month testing.

> *Storytime: "Testing Limits" First day of testing and my neighbor and I are both greeting our students as they walk into our classrooms. It's no surprise that state testing is happening today, we have been talking about it for the last two weeks. The differences in our classroom environments are drastic. I observe my neighbors' students enter her classroom quietly and head straight to their desks. My students are surrounding my door like moths to a flame asking questions such as "Are we testing today? "Will I be able to use the bathroom?" "Are we going to eat lunch? "How many math problems are there?" "Do I have to take the test?" You get the picture. It takes me a total of forty-five minutes to get my students quiet and actually begin taking their tests. After 15 minutes of making my rounds to check in and see that they're all on task, I turn to reheat my coffee when three hands go in the air. Each one asks to use the bathroom. Part of the testing procedures (which we've gone over many times) is to only allow one student at a time to leave the classroom for any reason. Students must also be chaperoned by an adult while in the hallway. This simple request to use the restroom also requires that their tests be suspended while away from their computer. It's a tedious process to say the least. After tracking down an adult to escort my kiddos one at a time (which took a total of 30 minutes), I start the clock on how long each test is suspended. I can only suspend a test for fifteen minutes. Luckily, everyone is back within the allotted time frame. Now's a good time for that coffee of mine, right? Wrong. I now have two students who claim to have finished their tests while two others are fast asleep.*

Needless to say, my reasons for ignoring the student who asked to use his calculator on his phone required no explanation. (I've already covered this question during the scripted directions). Without coffee, I finally begin to settle in my chair to check my emails. The first one I open is from my neighbor. She felt the need to tell me that her students appear to be taking their test very seriously. She also shared how she's been able to catch up on some grading while watching a movie on her HBO phone app. Inner voice: *Ain't this some $#!T. This chick! Must be F#@%ing nice! * (but I maintain). Passive-aggressive response: "Good for you. Friendly reminder, Charlie's IEP meeting is scheduled for Wednesday. You can email me his progress notes this afternoon. Happy grading!"

Amidst all the testing, we are still required to teach. When, you ask? During the last few minutes we have in the afternoon of course. This is when we squeeze in a 2-hour modified schedule that includes lunch, recess, a math, AND reading lesson as well as fluency interventions. My sympathy goes towards the newbie who has her observation scheduled during the month of April. Rookie mistake, assuming students will be better behaved and willing to participate during testing month.

To sum it up, the month of April, quite frankly tests my patience. April is long with no breaks in sight. Students and teachers are tested to within an inch of their sanities and the desire for summer vacation grows by the minute. When a teacher you know comes home with a messy bun, frequent migraines, and an untucked shirt, be weary, testing season is in full bloom.

May-Finish Line

Ah, MAY! Oh how I've missed you. I love being reunited with the month of May. May always brings me such joy. It lets me know, I made it! May rejuvenates me with the same level of energy I came in with. The end of the school year is unmatched. We are gearing up for promotions and summer vacations. With the end in sight, the energy has shifted from high intensity to serenity with the flip of a calendar page. Eighth graders are deciding on promotion outfits while teachers are booking their flights out of dodge. It's the first time all year that teachers and students are all on the same page and are sharing a common goal: make it to the last day of school.

End of year tasks include finalizing report cards, updating IEP goals, submitting last minute paperwork, and cleaning and organizing my classroom. Those bulletin boards I was so anxious to post are now being carefully dismantled (in case there is something I can reuse), desks are having name tags removed (ready for the crop of students next year), and the white board is getting the best (possibly first) cleaning it has had all year. During this time, I tend to reflect on what the school year has brought. While most of the year feels like a blur, some high and low points do stick out.

The low points of the school year obviously include the student behaviors I needed to address on a daily. The Devious lick challenges and classroom flying drones are two examples of what I could've done without all year. But hey, if it didn't happen and my students were perfect, then I wouldn't have anything to write about! And let's not forget about some of those adult errors on "what not to do" in education. Did I ever mention the story of when my assistant principal decided to "model" for me on how to deescalate an unsafe student? Well, I learned that it's NOT by arguing and ripping your coat jacket off to place a student in a safety restraint for 60 seconds. This was followed by a directive from my A.P. telling me to take over so that he may attend a meeting. Before you start to think that I am making sh*t up at this point because I ran out of material…I promise you that is not the case. I know that we can count the errors in this scenario, but I used it as a teaching tool. My dad has always said that no one is useless, they can always be used as a bad example. I applied this to help mold me into the educator that I am. These experiences have also guided me in avoiding turning into a leader who is frowned upon. This should go without saying but never put a child in a safety hold unless SAFETY is a concern. Veteran teachers know how to avoid these types of power struggles. They NEVER work out and will end up making you look like a fool. Hence, my administrator walking out, leaving me to pick up the pieces. But enough about the low points and poor leadership examples, let's hit those high notes.

The ability to watch my students flourish throughout the school year is amazing. When that light bulb goes on and you witness that "ah ha" moment towards a skill that they were otherwise convinced couldn't learn, is music to my ears. Also, at the top of my playlist, are the returning students. These are the students who come back year after year. They stop by just to say "hi" or invite me to their upcoming birthday, quicenera and/or wedding. Yes, I've been doing this a long time! What really hits that G10 note for me are the caring and supportive relationships I've built along the way. I have had the honor to work alongside individuals who've treated me like family, loved me like a sister, celebrated my triumphs and supported me through some of my darkest hours. Focusing back to concluding the school year, in some ways, it marks the end of a version of myself.

Storytime: "The Graduate" As you know, my sister and I share the same profession. What you may not know, is that we worked in the same district for several years allowing us to share some of the same students. One specific student that sticks out is a success story that my sister and I can both share. The day that I met "Mikey", he walked into my classroom utterly confused and said "Mrs. Lizarraga?" Obviously, he was confusing me with my sister who was his former teacher from his elementary school the previous year. After answering "Yes, she is my sister" for the hundredth time, (there were several other former students of hers), I was able to introduce myself and begin class. Having the same group of kiddos for their entire middle school years, I'm able to watch them grow and mature. Like with anything else in life, time flies by, and these kiddos were now going to be graduating high school. Our middle school holds their eighth-grade promotion ceremony at the neighboring high school where most of our promoting students will attend. Promotion day, like every other year, I'm outside the auditorium getting the promoting class in alphabetical order. (ABC's are still a struggle people!) I felt a tap on my shoulder. I turn to see "Mikey" standing there in his ROTC uniform with a huge smile on his face (as he always did). He immediately bent down to give me a hug, (he's over six feet tall) and filled me in on his future after high school. "Mikey" is a senior and will be graduating next week. With much enthusiasm, he explained how he was going out of state on a full athletic football scholarship and thanked my sister and I for that. I looked at him confused and reminded him that it was his athletic skills that got him that scholarship, not us. It's no surprise, but my sister and I are not knowledgeable in football. He laughed and said that "because of everything that you guys taught me, I was able to stay on the football team all four years." I'm not going to lie, but he had me at HELLO! I was so choked up I could barely get the words "thank you" out of my mouth. "Mikey" hugged and thanked me again before turning away to get ready for the Color Guard Presenting of the Flags ceremony. And there went the water works. I stood there with tears trickling down my cheeks. In that moment, I felt like the most honored, humbled, and effective teacher that I've ever been. I quickly gathered my thoughts, refocused my attention and began to reteach the alphabet to our promoting eight grade class.

Every year I receive a new batch of kiddos with a new batch of needs. My previous years' classroom management strategies may not necessarily be a good fit for the current classroom students. I, like most teachers, am constantly reinventing myself so that I am always presenting my best version. It's no easy task and it's not for the uncreative. Approaching the end of the school year, I put the latest version of myself away to be used again when the opportunity presents itself. After the promotion certificates are distributed and that bell chimes for one last time, I'm reminded that… we've made it to the finish line.

June—Wash, Rinse, Repeat

S chools...out...for...summer! It's SUMMERTIME. Time to break out our sunscreen and passports and travel to far away exotic places and rejuvenate. I'm totally kidding. Most teachers, like myself, work over the summer to prepare for the next school year. Curriculum planning, behavior management trainings, and any other professional developments that meet our 301 requirements fill up quickly. The myth that teachers are paid over the summer is exactly that, a myth. Teachers work year-round to not only make ends meet, but to also be proactive for the next school year. Education is a living organism and is constantly changing. We need to make sure that we can keep up with these changes. The passports and sunscreen will just have to wait.

Attending professional development trainings over summer has its own vibe. We are all more relaxed and have replaced our hot coffees and granola bars for iced teas and salads. Maxi skirts, dresses, shorts, and sandals replace the school logo tee's, slacks, and closed toed shoes. Working with my colleagues over the summer is about enjoyable productivity. We are all at ease and feeling a sense of accomplishment for making it through another school year. The purpose of extended summer work is to assist in making the upcoming school year less stressful and more seamless. I know that whatever next year brings, I won't be completely ready for it. Do you think we were prepared for a global pandemic? Trust me, that was not a typical drill that we've been preparing for, unlike our lockdown and fire drills. Though it's something to continue to consider for the future. That's the beauty of education and teaching. Every day is different and unscripted.

> *Storytime: "Lost in Space" It's the first week in June and I'm already sitting in a training for next year. Sigh. This time, it's because I'm in need of 301 hours. What are 301 hours?? 301 hours are 15 clock hours of professional development accumulated each year that the state requires for teaching certification. Yep, this means we need to complete MORE PD outside of the required trainings that are provided throughout the school year by the district. The positive outcome to this requirement: Free Choice! I can study basket weaving and get credit if I wanted to. My choice this summer: Mission to Mars. Based on the last school year's shenanigans, this felt suitable. Am I ever going to utilize this in my classroom? No, and here's why. The Mars education program provides opportunities for teachers to join with scientists and assist the research process of Mars. We are asked questions like, "Why is it that we find significant evidence of water flows on Mars but, we also know that Mars is too cold to sustain water flows?" While this is a great posing question, I am currently a Special Education teacher for elementary school students. We focus on reading, writing, and math. The only research we will be doing in my class is on Wikipedia about the stages of a butterfly's life. I will leave college level courses to people with the last name of Einstein. As invigorating as this subject is, I'm discreetly eyeing the crystals that are for sale and thinking about how I can transform them into jewelry. Just so you know, the Carnelian gem stones that I purchased will make for a lovely necklace and bracelet set.*

The remainder of my summer vacation (all three weeks of it) will consist of completing the many at home projects that have been neglected all school year. While I don't have to adhere to a bell schedule over summer, my time is instead controlled by my children and their many extracurricular activities. From traveling between music classes, softball games and reproducing the latest home organizational trend I saw on TicTok, I manage to book a four-day family trip to the happiest place on Earth, DISNEYLAND! For four glorious days I am decked out in Mickey gear and comfy shoes. I stand in hour long lines for rides, churros, and parades to watch the night skies light up with their firework displays. This trip takes me back to being a tween and helps channel my inner child while I hum the latest Disney tune.

As vacations often tend to fly by, I find myself back at home unpacking my many novelty souvenirs, catching up on laundry (as always), and ordering take out. Who wants to cook after a vacation? NOT it! Tonight's dinner, pepperoni pizza. As I wait for "Dan" to deliver my pizza, I begin writing my shopping list for my next Target run (I can't wait to give Ashley her Disney souvenir).

I step out to check the mail and wait for my pizza. In the mailbox, I come across that one dreaded envelope addressed to me: our Welcome Back letter. I was hoping to avoid that letter for at least one more week. Glancing at the calendar on my phone, the letter's right on time, and so is Dan with my pizza. I walk back inside, set the pizza to the side, and turn to the letter with despair. I unfold it and place it front and center on my refrigerator. This is so I don't "accidentally" forget the "Save the Date" memo of when to return. In the fridge, a chilled bottle of wine. I snatch the bottle from the side door of the refrigerator and quickly turn to my couch where it's waiting for me to settle in and cue to Netflix. I try my hardest to keep focus on the NCIS marathon and stare into the television only to picture: The Letter! The date of the letter is etched into my brain. In just a weeks' time, I will be back on campus preparing for another school year. Like the shampoo bottle says, for best results; wash, rinse, repeat.

About the Author's

Mary Lizarraga was born and raised in Phoenix, Arizona. Mary has been an educator for 22 years, serving as a special education teacher, mentor, and administrator. During this time, she has had the opportunities to work with special needs populations, culturally and linguistically diverse individuals and community-based organizations. Mary currently resides in Arizona with her husband of 23 years and their two daughters.

Cheryl Culver is also a special educator residing in Phoenix Arizona with her husband and two children. She currently works as a behavior specialist in an inner-city school. Cheryl has worked in the educational field in a variety of roles for the last 10 years and looks forward to many more.

This is their first book. What started out as facetime banter soon flourished into chapter titles. As sisters Mary and Cheryl hope to capture their audience's attention through real life experiences and sarcastic humor involving topics such as motherhood, marriage, and many more.